*A Journey of a Lifetime:*
*Breaking Free from Religion's Box*

# MESSAGES
## FROM

**BALBOA**.PRESS

A DIVISION OF HAY HOUSE

Balboa Press books may be ordered through booksellers or by contacting:

Balboa Press
A Division of Hay House
1663 Liberty Drive
Bloomington, IN 47403
www.balboapress.com
1 (877) 407-4847

Print information available on the last page.

ISBN: 978-1-9822-4699-0 (sc)
ISBN: 978-1-9822-4701-0 (hc)
ISBN: 978-1-9822-4700-3 (e)

Library of Congress Control Number: 2020908436

Balboa Press rev. date: 05/26/2020

This book is dedicated to my fellow truth seekers who are out there searching to find "The Way." The way that makes their hearts sing with love, peace, freedom, and joy.

I give thanks and immense gratitude to my Father in heaven for using me as an instrument to allow his divine words of wisdom to flow through me onto the paper. I am grateful to my personal divine posse for showing up every day of my life to help guide and protect me.

I am grateful for all the authors who have dedicated their lives to follow their dharma and write beautiful books that allow us the opportunity to read, search, and consequently develop our own personal spiritual philosophy.

I am grateful for my wonderful family and friends, who have always been supportive of my spiritual journey, even though our perspectives were not always the same.

I am grateful for all the many, many diverse experiences that I have had in my life that allowed me to create this book with true empathy and compassion and ultimately led me to hear my Father's voice within.

And lastly, I am grateful for everyone at Balboa Press who had a hand in making my manuscript come to life in book form.

# CONTENTS

# PREFACE

Everyone's life takes them on their own unique journey. Personal growth and awareness come from dedicated personal work and introspective study to unravel the amnesia that we are born into life with. This material is not meant to be a religious point of view, a source of intricate counseling, or the be all and end all of information. I am simply sharing my own personal story, which led me to create an outlook on life and ultimately a spiritual philosophy that resonates deep within my soul. It allows me to live life with unconditional love and understanding for all people, places, and things. My hope is that it may help open your eyes to a perspective that leads you on your own personal quest to create a perspective of your own. It is meant to encourage and inspire your own awakening. It has been a journey of a lifetime for me, filled with a vast number of experiences and a lot of soul-searching to create it. No matter what stage you are in life, gaining a positive perspective will propel you in the right direction. May this book help ignite the spark of God within you, which in turn will stimulate your search for truth and ultimately help you find your real identity. You will know that you're headed in the right direction by how you feel. As I repeat throughout the book, take that which feels good to you, and discard that which does not. We are all on individual journeys; this is solely meant to spark the curiosity within, leading you on a trajectory to find how to live a life filled with happiness and joy and to help change the lens you view life with in a beautiful and positive way. As Wayne Dyer puts it, "Change the way you look at things, and the things you look at change."

By the end of *Messages from Love*, may you achieve this accomplishment. You will find that everything you need, you already have; it's just a matter of tapping into what's already there and consequently finding it that starts the whole ball rolling. The good news is that it's so very simple. Life really is, very simple.

Blessings to you all on starting and experiencing your own personal journey of a lifetime.

# INTRODUCTION

For as long as I can remember, I've been trying to figure out who I am. My journey in this incarnation has been filled with an extensive variety of experiences from as far back as I can remember. I started to do a lot of self-reflecting as I approached the age of fifty. I remember thinking to myself that all these experiences had given me a tremendous sense of understanding, compassion, and empathy for others. I could relate in so many different ways with so many different experiences people would talk to me about. I often found myself in conversations that were therapy oriented. I found that I was drawn to helping others with this immense feeling, desire, and almost need for others to be happy themselves. I have spent much of my adult life in this role, trying to help or fix others so they could be happy in their life. I realize now, after years and years of studying the big questions in life, that my need to help others was really my own personal need to fulfill this in myself. If I could get others to successfully find their bliss, I would have the opportunity to share that feeling with them.

In this last decade, I decided I needed to change how I was living and retreated into a sort of cocoon state. I was becoming aware that the happiness I was searching for with others needed to be cultivated in myself. I had spent so much of my life helping others that I didn't even know who I was. I created a safe environment in my home, which I now call my "bubble world," and proceeded to spend years cultivating a space that felt like heaven on earth to me. It was the only place I wanted to be. As I learned, grew, and filled myself up through the introspective spiritual work I was doing, I had many amazing synchronistic and ethereal experiences.

One by one, they lifted the veil of the earthly illusion, which allowed me to see myself in a way that finally resonated deep within my soul. Those years were life-changing for me. As my cocoon matured and opened, I came out on the other side feeling like a new person. The lens through which I now view life sees much clearer. I have a newfound perspective that allows me to live life with peace and freedom; it's incredibly beautiful, kind, and loving. This perspective is all-encompassing, with an understanding and allowance for all my fellow brothers and sisters who are on their own individual journey of a lifetime. We are all walking this path in our own way, perfectly entangled, to teach each other through our interconnectedness. We are learning in this earth school through the basis of opposites. This gives us the opportunity to learn what feels good and what does not.

Through this trajectory, we make choices, and the outcome of our choices creates a feeling. We are in charge of our lives by the choices we make and the road our choices lead to create an outcome. There are no wrong or bad choices because every choice allows us to feel one way or another; this is how we learn. We are the creators of our lives, for we are each individual sparks of God, a part of the collective energy of the Great I Am. When we learn and remember who we really are, when we tap into the infinite power of the Christ consciousness within, we tap into the feeling of home.

Our brother known as Jesus was the first to achieve this goal. His life was a gift to humanity and created an example of what we are trying to achieve in this life. He is with us all by the mere asking to know him in our hearts and in our lives. His guidance is available to everyone with a desire to know him. We are at the beginning stages of the New Earth. Mother Earth is restless and creating anew. A spiritual awakening is happening all over the world at this time as she transitions. We see her unsettledness through the unrest in our weather patterns and the sort of craziness in society as a whole. We are moving into an age of perfect peace and love, literally creating heaven on earth. Those who are ready to make this shift will experience a transition in their Self and in their life.

This is what the church and religious institutions call the Second Coming. I personally believe the Second Coming is here right now. We have a choice to hop on board and move into the New Earth by how we conduct ourselves every day, doing the work to understand and participate in life with love, peace, and nonjudgment, with the understanding that everyone does this work at their own pace, in their own way, with their own timing. As we move forth with unconditional love, we free ourselves from the bondage of the old earthly ways and energy. We create a new energy of light and find our spark within that matches the light and vibration of our Father in heaven. The result is living on earth as it is in heaven, creating heaven on earth.

# INCEPTION OF THE EPISODES

I came to a point in my life where the information in the thirteen episodes seemed to be literally bursting out of my soul. At this point, I had been in a very introspective period for many years, studying religion, spirituality, and the big questions of life: Why are we here, and what is our purpose?

Being an intense and avid truth seeker, I realized that my life had led me on an extensive journey with a vast array of experiences that included many different people, places, and things. These experiences gave me a tremendous amount of understanding and compassion for others. As I reflected with hindsight, I innately knew that it was for a deeper purpose other than just the experiences themselves. Right before the age of fifty, I found myself yearning to be by myself; I went into sort of a cocoon state, so to speak. I continued to perform my morning ritual, which I had been doing for years: I would wake up very early in the morning to read my spiritual books, watch videos on religion and spirituality, and engage in hours of prayer and meditation. It was then that I noticed a voice that seemed to be talking back to me. This voice was always so kind, loving, and wise. I began to really pay attention; I knew that these messages I was receiving needed to be written down. I proceeded to write these messages almost every morning for about a year. These messages became what I call Messages from Love.

Once these messages were compiled, I tried to take a break from the intense study but often found myself feeling unwell. I seemed to catch the next illness or virus that was going around, and my energy level was extremely low. At the same time, I had a few intense experiences that led me to feeling like I needed to retire after almost thirty years as an aesthetician. I was consumed by the idea of writing a book, but I didn't have a clue where to start. I felt like there were years of information stuffed inside me, screaming to get out. I didn't talk to many people about my spiritual quest; it was something I did in my alone time.

Over the next two years, I attempted two different times to retire and change my life, so I could concentrate on writing a book about all I had learned. To my dismay it never work out; the doors kept slamming, and it never made financial sense.

At the peak of feeling really run down, our family had planned a weeklong vacation in Tahoe. It ended up being an amazing week with different family members coming in and out, and beautiful morning conversations on the balcony among the gorgeous pine trees with the outside fireplace lit (my favorite thing to do). My niece, who was attending college at Reno University, was staying with us; she had been struggling with her own place in her spiritual life. Every morning, she and I had deep and lengthy conversations. She had taken a class on podcasts and editing and found that she not only had a passion for it but was very talented at doing them. So one morning, after talking for about four hours, she brought up the fact she had a class in the fall where she needed material to put a podcast and website together; she suggested that we use some of the writings that I had done for it. I said absolutely; I really had no idea what that would entail, but I readily agreed, and we left it at that.

Fast forward a few months. One Friday in October, out of the blue, she reached out to me and said, "Okay, I'm ready to start the podcast. I need the first episode by Monday."

I didn't have a clue what she needed from me, but I innately knew it was an opportunity I needed to seize. In addition, to make things more complicated, she wanted this first episode to be all about me. I had spent the last seven years in a very introspective state, journaling and gaining a deeper understanding of myself, but that was not what I thought the focus would be on.

With that said, I did understand the importance of creating a foundation of where the writings of Messages from Love were derived from. So I stressed out all weekend but did write the first episode and shared it with her, only to have her say, "Okay, now I need you to voice it. Go into your closet, use the voice app on your phone, and record what you wrote."

What?

Everything she was asking me to do was so far out of my comfort zone. Again, though, I knew I needed to follow through; I knew it would put me on a trajectory that would start the ball rolling to share this information that was stuck inside of me, screaming to get out. So I did as she asked and accomplished the task.

I sent her the recording and waited a couple of unsettling days, and then I got a response from her. She proceeded to text me the first episode, complete with her voice and prologue, my voiced episode, and an epilogue in her words, all done to music. I was amazed at how beautiful it was. That opened the floodgates for me, and I proceeded to write a total of thirteen episodes in a very short period of time. She only needed three for her class project, but I couldn't stop writing. The more I wrote, the better I felt. By the time the thirteenth episode was complete, I felt like a new person, like a weight had been lifted off my shoulders.

I decided to leave each episode of Messages from Love in its original format for this book. My hope is that you find the words to be as kind, loving, and beautiful to read as I experienced when receiving them; I hope they inspire your own magical journey of a lifetime.

Thank you for this opportunity and your time as a reader, and may God bless your lives with peace.

I will end with a Message from Love, entitled "The Door of Everything."

# The Door of Everything

My Father, with you and only you are we able to experience heaven on earth, living on earth as it is in heaven. As we walk this life, traveling down the road on our own unique journey, all experiences lead back to you. We're trying to figure out how to find love, peace, and joy every day in this experience on earth. What are your words of wisdom for us, my Father?

*"My children come into this life solely to remember who they really are; to find me within them; and to experience life, love, and forgiveness through faith. All of you will do this in your own way. Every way is perfect. It is through your free will that you may stumble and fall and simultaneously rise up with success on your ultimate journey, which leads you back to your roots, your truth—you are a spiritual being in a human body, experiencing life in a very low and dense vibrational atmosphere."*

*"One day, you will find me within the likes of you. Then, we will rise up and out of the dark, dense vibration into a higher, magical vibration, which exists only for those who work very hard to climb their way out of the dark and into the light. This is only done in quiet stillness, alone with me. At this point, the Door of Everything becomes your opportunity to open and walk through with me, and your life will never be the same. The journey then begins, and the synchronicities magically start to propel your life anew."*

*"Each amazing experience helps your faith become stronger and allows you to move forward, open your heart, and trust; you begin to realize that there's a whole lot more going on in this existence than meets the eye. This, my love, is faith and truth working in your life to give you inner strength and telling you that you're not alone, that your reason for being here is based not on the illusion you see with your naked eye, which appears to be truth, but on the real truth of life, which is seen with new eyes. These eyes give you new insight; you see beyond the illusionary veil and find that we are, and have always been, connected as one. As you continue to climb the mountain with me, your life takes on a new glory, creating a thirst that continuously needs quenching. At this point, you are on a continuum of learning and growing, perfectly and beautifully on time and on purpose for the growth of your soul. Enjoy the journey. It is meant to be exalting, one day at a time, one step at a time, and love, peace, and joy become your new reality."*

# CHAPTER 1

## EPISODE 1

## Divine Connection

I would like to start by giving you a brief synopsis of my spiritual journey in order to help you understand where I've come from and what has brought me to this conversation today.

I was born into a beautiful family as the middle child of three. My childhood memories are wonderful, and I have always been grateful for the gift of being born into a family filled with kindness and love. I was raised in a family that followed a strict organized religion. It was our life and created a firm foundation of good morals and values. It was my first experience in learning about God and Jesus. When I got older, I often became aware of feelings that weren't always comfortable. The doctrine I was being taught didn't always resonate with me. As I prepared at a young age for my baptism, I innately wished I had been a convert; I would therefore be a member because I had chosen it.

As I grew older, I became restless and rebelled a bit in my teenage years, yearning to stretch my wings and find my own way. When I was old enough to make my own decisions, I chose not to be involved with the church any longer and set out on my way. I initially enjoyed living without the confines of structures and rules. I felt a sense of freedom in living as I chose, not as I was told. This set into motion a quest that has lasted my whole life, searching for what I deemed to be truth and creating freedom in all areas of my life. Through many different experiences, good, bad, and everything in between, I created a belief system that is all my own. I believe in a truth that feels right for me after extensive studying, reading, praying, and then listening. Listening to that voice within my head, I suddenly realized it has been with me for as long as I could remember: the beautiful and exquisite voice of God. The belief system I have now come to believe as true is from years and years of searching and studying, ultimately leading me to find my direct connection with God, who is not just some figure in the sky, but we as spirits in a human body are directly connected to God and have the spark of God within us. We truly are one with him.

We've all heard the sayings, "Ask and ye shall receive" and "You are never alone for I am with you always." This is because we are directly connected to God in our hearts and in our souls, through the very air that we breathe and the very blood that flows through our veins. We learn to know and feel his presence as pure and unconditional love. We eventually learn that all that is good is of God, and anything other than good is not of him. It is just that simple.

I encourage you to take the time each day to cultivate your own relationship with God. It's the only way to ultimately create a belief system that works for you individually. Not because you have been told what to believe but because you have searched and found your truth directly with the Creator of all, our Father in heaven, God, source, energy, the universe, a higher power; all terms reflect God. Choose what feels right for you; he answers to all. For the purpose of speaking about God, I will often use the word "He." With that said, I fully know God as the source of all things, of everything there is, the Great I Am.

A few years ago, my daughter sent me an untitled poem written by an unknown author. I read it and realized that it was the perfect description of who I am at my core. It goes like this:

> I have the deepest affection for intellectual conversations. The ability to just sit and talk. Talk about love, talk about life, talk about anything and talk about everything. To sit under the moon with all the time in the world. The full-speed train, that is our lives, slowing to a crawl. Bound by no obligations, barred by no human

limitations. To speak without regret or fear of consequence.

And to talk for hours about what's really important in life.

Author Unknown

I have had the wonderful opportunity in my life to enjoy going on many vacations with family and friends. Anyone who has vacationed with me knows that my favorite time of the day is when we wake up in the morning, grab a cup of coffee, and either head out to the patio to enjoy the warm morning air or stay cuddled inside next to the fireplace and have amazing conversation. We could talk for hours pondering life's big questions, resolving issues in our own lives, discussing our latest epiphanies in spiritual philosophies, and then finish with how to create love, peace, and happiness all around us.

When I'm not on vacation, I'm usually blessed with a schedule that allows me to do the same thing on my own: wake up, grab my coffee, head back to bed, prop my pillows, and proceed to read my newest favorite spiritual book, pray, meditate, and then listen. Listen to the morning message that comes through, in my mind. One morning recently, a message was coming through that I didn't want to forget, so I broke my meditative state and grabbed my phone to write it down in my notes.

As I did, the message seemed to keep flowing, and my fingers couldn't go fast enough. It finally came to a halt, and when I read it back, I couldn't believe the beauty in the words that had come through; it seemed to be written as if God were speaking to me. I felt as if it was the most beautiful, loving, and kind message that could only come from the purest source of unconditional love. Tears rolled down my cheeks, and gratitude filled my heart; the experience was completely overwhelming.

The next morning, I woke and proceeded to do my morning routine; I wondered if it would happen again. Sure enough, the same experience, but with a new subject. Again, the most beautiful words of wisdom. This continued for about a year, on and off, depending on what was going on in my life.

One day, I decided to print all my writings, fearing that if I lost my phone, they would all be gone. As I printed note after note, I was amazed at how much information had come through. I now call these essays Messages from Love. My intention in doing these podcasts is to share these messages with you. I hope they will touch your heart as deeply and profoundly as they do mine. Some of them are written as if God is speaking to you, and others are written as beautiful words of wisdom on a particular life subject.

Please take that which feels good to you, and discard that which does not. This life we live is our own individual journey, and what's most important is to live our truth and be our most authentic self. We, with God, are the masters of our lives here in this earthly realm.

Always listen to the song in your heart, follow only what feels right for you, and give the gift of honoring each of your fellow brothers and sisters in their individual journey as well; the journey of a lifetime is all about love, compassion, and forgiveness.

I will end with a Message from Love, entitled "Patiently I Wait."

. . . . . . . . . . . . . . . . . . . . . . . . . . . . . . . . . . . . . . . . . . . . . . . . . . . . . . . . . . . . . . . . . . . . .

# Patiently I Wait

*"At the dawn of each new day, always remember the gift, the gift that renews itself 365 days a year, a fresh start to see the world with eyes of love and the opportunity to stand in awe of its beauty. Your world has progressed over the centuries, decades, and generations exactly on time and on purpose for the understanding of finding yourself anew. Different time periods have brought different things to the table, but the common thread that stays steadfast throughout the millennia is the search for God."*

*"The journey for each of my children is their own and unique to them. But in the end, it's all the same: the search to fill that yearning within. Spirituality is a personal quest to find God within your heart and soul on your own. Religion is for those who may desire the boundaries and confines of theology and doctrine, which is taught to them as truth. Each of these avenues lead my children to me. But the only way to find me within you is to know me personally. Not as a man somewhere in the heavens who judges and expects perfection. But to know me within the heart of you and to know that my love is kind, forgiving, and understanding."*

*"There will always be another opportunity to get it right; however, the journey is to be played out with the ultimate knowledge that I, as your Father in heaven, am experiencing this with you, waiting in the background until*

you bring me forth into the forefront. Then in that instant, we walk together. This is when your experience in this life changes from confusion and darkness to clarity and simplicity."

"As you continue to commune with me, a new journey begins. Your eyes suddenly see the amazing beauty in all things and in all people, and as you continue down the path with me in your heart, your heart then sings with the joy it is meant to feel. We then walk and talk until your time on earth comes to an end, and you transition back home to me, more enlightened with a little more clarity. As always, all is well."

# CHAPTER 2

## EPISODE 2

# In the Beginning

As we move forward on this journey, I would like to emphasize the importance of checking in with yourself as you read these chapters. Please note that this material is not meant to replace any religious or spiritual beliefs you already have; it's an avenue to expand your knowledge, explore new perspectives, and possibly enhance what you already know. I will often use repetition throughout the book for the purpose of understanding a concept more fully. I will also use stories, metaphors, and parables for this same purpose. Be aware of how it feels when receiving the different ideas that I introduce. Again, this is the philosophy that I have compiled, and it feels right for me.

As I said earlier, take that which feels right to you; discard that which does not. God has placed within us all a beautiful gift: a barometer that allows us to feel, one way, or another. This personal barometer allows you to create your own spiritual philosophy. Let us start now from the beginning, using a metaphor to understand the concept.

Once upon a time, God, the Creator of all, decided to expand himself and burst into millions of pieces, creating us. He placed a piece of himself in each and every one of his creations. He proceeded to create earth, a beautiful place for them to live for the purpose of experiencing life in every possible way. In each and every one of us is a piece of the Creator, a spark of God. This spark is the beautiful, kind, and loving voice that we hear in our head, the sweet and compassionate feeling we sense in our heart. When we learn to pay attention to it and decipher it from the negative voice and feeling of ego, we realize that we have a constant companion that serves us and guides us every second of every day.

This explains why we are told we only have to ask and we will receive, because at any given moment of any given day, he is with us. He actually resides within us, ready and waiting for us to just ask him to come forth. He speaks to us not only in an audible way but also by the way we feel. If we stay tuned and connected to the way we feel, get quiet enough to calm down the chatter in our head, we realize we have a divine presence speaking to us constantly. This voice is beautiful, kind, loving, helpful, uplifting, and always sweet. For God is pure, unconditional love.

He loves each and every one of his creations, his children, the same. He wants only the very best for us, for each and every one of us is an emanation of him. To make things more intriguing, complicated, and exciting, we are given amnesia when we enter this journey called life. We are born with amnesia and spend the rest of our lives trying to remember who we really are, to find him again, within our being, when all along, he has always been with us, speaking loud and clear as a prominent voice within our head. He leads and guides us through our joys and elations as well as our trials and tribulations. Typically for most, there comes a juncture in our lives where the times get tough, and we find ourselves down on our knees asking, sometimes begging, for him to show up and help.

All the while, however, he has been with us, in all ways, waiting patiently for us to find him. At the point we find him within, we finally breathe a sigh of relief because at this moment, we realize we are not alone. We are then ready to receive His gifts, his gifts of peace, his gifts of love, his gifts of compassion, kindness, and beauty. We learn the art of forgiveness and nonjudgment. There is a beautiful art in reciprocity, in the giving and receiving of loving and serving others. We begin to fully understand the concept that all that is good is of God, just by the mere awareness of his presence within. Our light, his light begins to radiate from our being. At this point, all that is asked of us is to shine his light and represent his goodness in all that we do and all that we are. We should set an example for our fellow brothers and sisters, to help them find him in their lives as well.

Thus, his movement spreads like a welcoming light that all will gravitate toward, because why? Simply said, it feels good.

I personally believe that Jesus came to this earthly realm to teach us this, as God's perfect Son, in a human body, the perfect protocol of man. We are all sons and daughters of God. Jesus is our perfect brother, who came to set an example of how to live and connect with God, in all ways.

Jesus said, "All that I do, you too can do." He came to shine his light, God's light, and teach us to treat others, as well as ourselves, with love and respect. He taught the art of forgiveness under the most tragic and horrifying of circumstances. He taught humility and showed us that we, too, can have our own direct connection with God, our Father. Lastly and most significantly, through his resurrection, He taught us that we never really die, that our soul, our spirit, lives on for eternity.

We are all beautiful emanations of God. This life on earth is really his experiment to experience himself anew, in all ways, through us, his children. Jesus was his prime example, a gift to us all so that we would have a living example of what we are trying to achieve here. He's a beautifully perfect example and a tangible source to look up to, to guide us in this experience, this journey we call life.

This is why it is said that we can find our way through Jesus Christ. He taught us, through example, the way to get back home to our Father in heaven, our source, the Creator of the universe, God, who in reality has never left us; slowly but surely, the veil of illusion, that we are somehow separate from God, is lifted, and we remember that we are one. We are born into this world of illusion, this world of ego, gifted with the truth of God, the truth of our soul and spirit, but with amnesia. So what we see with our five senses is what we think is truth. In reality, what we see is an illusion, a smoke screen, covering the truth of our real identity and our true existence.

Again, we are all God's children, with his spark at the epicenter of our being. We may have amnesia to our truth, but the barometer he placed inside us, his gift, is there to help us navigate out of the darkness and illusion, into remembering who we really are. This is all done through how we feel. The term used for a strong feeling or perception is *clairsentience,* more commonly known as our sixth sense, or intuition.

Some are more in touch with their sixth sense than others. Some are born into this world with the gift of a strong sense of intuition. These people, I believe, have come to earth at this particular time to help assist in the awakening, to help our fellow brothers and sisters lift the smoke screen of illusion and usher in the reawakening of truth and light, God's truth and light.

This awakening will help change the trajectory of society's current climate of disaster, violence, hate, and destruction. Change it into love, peace, unity, and joy, the basis of who we are at our core. We are offered assistance, if we so choose, by these individuals who seem closely connected to the heavenly realm. Their sole life purpose, their dharma, is to help awaken our species at this critical time here on earth. They are leading an awakening out of the dense, dark vibration and illusion, into a higher vibration of truth, love, and light.

There is an imaginary bridge that spans the gap between heaven and the earthly realm. We can live heaven on earth, as it is in heaven. When we choose to remember, choose to go on the journey and ask for divine assistance, our life takes on a miraculous shift, a shift where the veil of illusion, the smoke screen, starts to dissolve, and God's light and love penetrate the darkness. The veil lifts little by little as we search. Seek and ye shall find, and your body and soul start to remember what is real. And what is real is that we are love; the only thing that is real is love. Anything other than love is an illusion of this earthly realm, and to climb out from the darkness, we simply remember that love is all there is. This is the purpose of our journey: to find God within and experience love.

I will end with a Message from Love, entitled "The Gift of Love."

## The Gift of Love

*"Never stray from my love. It is with you; it is within you. It is the you of you that is connected to me. Together we are one, experiencing life on earth, learning love, living love, and spreading love. Allow your heart to love all things and all people, and love is what you'll experience in return. Love even those who may seem unlovable, because your love for them brings them love as well. When people act without love, they have had a lack thereof and have*

*forgotten who they really are. Freely give your love to them, for it's the only gift that is worthwhile. Teach them, show them, and allow them to experience beautiful, unconditional love. I use my children for this purpose, the purpose of giving love to those who may be in the dark. May we change the darkness into light. May we fill those with an empty reservoir with joy. You are my light and my love, always and forever. Together, let's bless anyone and everyone who comes into your space with the joy that only this gift of unconditional love brings."*

# CHAPTER 3

## EPISODE 3

## Creating a Personal Relationship with God

Here is a short story from one of my favorite spiritual books, *Journey of the Master*, by Eva Belle Werber.

· · · · · · · · · · · · · · · · · · · · · · · · · · · · · · · · · · · · · · · · · · · · · · · · · · · · · · · · · · · · · · · · · · · · · · · · · · · · · · · · · · · ·

### The Journey of the Soul

God came to my soul and said, "Let us go on a journey together." So we went into the night, and there was nothing in all the universe but my soul with God.

The night was crystal clear, the sky studded with a million stars. The air carried a fragrance as if all the flowers on earth had released their perfume for our pleasure. I laughed aloud from pure joy as Spirit and I went into the night. There was no pavement beneath our feet; it was as if we were walking on air. We sang together all the songs of the ages.

As we continued on, I asked God, "May we stop here, at the house of my friends, and take them with us on our happy journey?" So we came to a stop, and my friends joined us. I suddenly noticed that somehow, the music did not ring as clearly, and the fragrance from the flowers had faded.

My friends then said, "Let us stop here and take our other friends with us too." And so we did. We all sang together, but again I noticed that the music lacked the sweet harmony that God and I sang alone together. Eventually, a fog settled over the night, and the stars were lost behind a silken veil. The perfume of the flowers became so faint that we soon lost it all together. The air was heavy, and the road hard to walk.

The friends we had gathered pulled at me, saying, "Come, go our way; it is a good way to go." As I turned to go with them, I saw a dim light through the fog. It was the light of God, the same light within the soul that burns forever, waiting patiently for us to find it. At that moment, I had a great awakening; I broke away from my friends' clinging hands and went forth, free.

The light of God then became so bright; the fog lifted, and a world of beauty lay before me. Again, God spoke to my soul, saying, "When you journey forth with me, you must journey alone, for it is only as you disentangle yourself from the outward form of earthly things that you can make the journey back to the truth of your soul. Until you have made this journey alone with me, you are not fit to guide others on the path."

When I awoke, I had a great sense of peace and knew that in the still watches of the night, Spirit had taught my soul a great lesson.

The first time I read this little story, I could not grasp the concept of leaving behind friends and family along the path of learning to connect, develop, and climb the mountain, creating a relationship with God. It was so counterintuitive to everything I thought was right. I didn't understand the importance of taking the journey alone. As I continued my study and search for the truth, I began to understand that it was not selfish but necessary and the only way to truly find your own personal relationship with God. You cannot give to others what you do not have. I also learned that where you find Him is alone in the silence. As your desire within is sparked, a slow process begins to take shape. This process develops one concept at a time, one experience at a time, one baby step at a time.

Your journey typically starts with curiosity and a feeling that there must be more to this life than meets the eye. This creates a desire to understand more than you've been taught. It becomes an insatiable thirst to know the truth. As you begin to quench this thirst, you can't seem to get enough. Ironically, however, on time and on purpose, the synchronicities begin. The right person comes into your path and says just the right thing or suggests just the right book, or simply by the mere presence of their energy and vibration, your spark is lit. You begin to move forward and understand the key point that there's a Higher Power that cannot be seen with the naked eye. Slowly but surely, as you continue your search, the veil of illusion starts to lift just a little.

Continuing on spending time in prayer and meditation, you begin to create a relationship with this Higher Power. You begin to ask for intervention and receive signs that tend to validate what you are learning. This is God's way of showing you that you are on track. We are given the gift of free will, so the divine will not interfere unless we ask. You will learn that the answers always come, but in unconventional ways. We call these miracles and realize they could only come from the unseen realm. This is how we know that there is something out there that hears our pleas and responds. The process that begins to develop strengthens our faith and is the key ingredient on this path to higher consciousness.

One of my favorite definitions of *faith* is "taking the first step, even when you don't see the whole staircase." It is the substance of inner peace, and as it grows stronger, you begin to see life through a new lens, one of peace and love for everything and everybody. As you continue your spiritual work, life takes you on a magical journey filled with miracles and synchronicities that create a sense of awe. This sense of awe becomes a contagious feeling that drives you in your search for the truth. This process stimulates your spark of God, which lays dormant within until ignited. Once the fire is lit, the flame grows, and your life takes on a whole new meaning and direction. Thus, the awakening begins, and we remember who we really are: beautiful creations of God, a spirit, a soul made in his image, housed in this human suit called a body.

We realize that God is not just somewhere out there, that he is, in fact, everywhere, everything, and everybody. We are actually connected to everything, everybody, everywhere. The lens you see the world with changes. Your perspective changes, and the beautiful feeling of love permeates your being.

I will end with a Message from Love, entitled "Life's Big Illusion."

. . . . . . . . . . . . . . . . . . . . . . . . . . . . . . . . . . . . . . . . . . . . . . . . . . . . . . . . . . . . . . . . . . . . . . . . . . . . . . . . . .

## Life's Big Illusion

*"The big illusion in this life is that we are separate, that you are there, and I am here. I long for my children to remember this concept; it's the biggest*

*misconception in life. It is the basis of all unhappiness and confusion. The truth is that we are one, and I am joined within the soul of each and every one of you. There is nothing that I am that you are not, and because this is so, any and everything that is not of me is an illusion. As soon as my children remember and tap into that place inside where we are connected, their world will change. It will change in a way that always views life with eyes of love, kindness, compassion, and beauty. The freedom that this brings makes you soar with pleasure and happiness. Consequently, the end result is a life filled with peace, my ultimate gift to those who find me within. Stay tuned and connected to me daily. Spend time and talk with me, tune your ear to hear my beautiful, sweet low voice within your head. I am with you, always yearning to have you hear my guidance and feel my love. This communing daily creates a flow, and the miracles arrive. This pleases me, for as we give, we both receive. Go now, my child, and find me; see me in everything you do, in everything you are, and in everyone you meet. Share the magic of living a glorious life with me."*

# CHAPTER 4

## EPISODE 4

*Forgiveness*

In the early 1990s, at the beginning of my personal quest for the truth, I was given a book by Neil Donald Walsh called *Conversations with God*. His books were my first experience in the untangling of my organized religious upbringing and leading me into a new perspective, a perspective that allowed a sense of freedom within. It helped me shed, little by little, the guilt of not being perfect, teaching me that there is nothing that is right or wrong, because everything we experience is an opportunity to learn. I gained an understanding that everyone is here to learn through experiences the lessons of their choosing. We always have a choice when coming into a life here on earth and a predestined agenda.

There is a beautiful invisible web I like to call "the Tapestry of Life," intricately and perfectly woven. We all collectively help each other, teaching each other these particular lessons with and through our collective experiences. They are beautiful acts of reciprocity, and without exception, we are always each other's teachers. What we choose to do with them, however, is our own personal experience. Some may be deemed as good, some not so good, and in other cases, quite tragic. You may find yourself in a relationship, in whatever capacity it may be: family, friend, romantic, coworker, a collective community, or just a stranger who made an impact in a moment's time. These relationships are there exactly on time and on purpose for the opportunity to learn from each other and each other's experiences, all entangled in a divine and perfect web. Each interaction creates a reciprocal feeling. We learn life lessons through the way they make us feel. There is a simple but impactful parable in *Conversations with God* that helps us understand this concept. It is called "The Little Soul and the Sun." It goes this:

## The Little Soul and the Sun

Once upon a time, there was a little soul who said to God, "I know who I am; I am the light."

"That's right," God said with a smile.

The little soul then added, "Now that I know who I am, I would like to experience it. I want to feel what it feels like to actually be the light."

God replied, "Okay, but you must realize I have created nothing but the light, and so there is no easy way for you to experience yourself as who you are, since there is nothing that you are not. So the question is, how can you know yourself as the light, when you are amid the light; I have an idea. We'll surround you in darkness."

"Won't I be afraid?" asked the little soul.

"There is nothing to be afraid of, unless you choose to be afraid. Remember, we are just making it all up, pretending; it's just a game. In order to experience anything, the exact opposite has to appear. So when you are surrounded with the darkness, do not get mad and curse at it. Rather, be the light unto the darkness. It is then that you will experience who you really are and know how special you are."

"Is it okay to feel special?"

"Yes, but also remember that special does not mean better. Everyone is special in their own unique way, yet many have forgotten."

"I choose to be that part of special that is forgiveness."

"Okay, but there's one thing you should know about being forgiveness; there's no one to forgive because I have made everyone perfect. There is not a single soul in all creation less perfect than you. Everyone is learning this through their own experiences. The question is, who then to forgive?"

At that moment, a friendly soul stepped forward and said, "Not to worry, little soul. I will help you. I can give you something to forgive. I can come into your next lifetime and do something that you will have to forgive."

"Oh, thank you," exclaimed the little soul. "You would do that for me? You, who are such a being of utter light and perfection?"

"Yes," the friendly soul replied. "I would do it because I love you, and because you have done the same thing for me. We have helped each other many times before; you just don't remember. So I will come into your next lifetime and be the bad one this time, so you can experience yourself as the one who forgives."

"What will you do that will be so terrible?"

"We'll think of something,." said the friendly soul. "You are right about one thing, though; I will have to slow down my vibration and become very heavy to do this bad thing. I will have to pretend to be something very unlike myself. So I have but one favor to ask of you in return."

"Anything."

"In the moment that I do the worst thing you could possibly imagine, please remember who I really am."

"I promise," said the little soul. "I will always remember you as I see you right now."

"Good, because I will be pretending so hard that I will forget who I really am. So if you don't remember, I may not remember, and if we both forget, we will be lost. Then, we will need another soul to come along to remind us both."

"I won't forget. I will remember you; I promise. And I will thank you for bringing me this gift, the opportunity to experience myself as forgiveness."

And so the agreement was made, and the little soul went forth into a new lifetime to have the experience of being that part of special called forgiveness.

Through this story, we see how we come into and out of each other's lives to help one another learn and grow in our continuous climb to ultimately achieve and experience our divine goodness. Some of our greatest teachers are often those we see as our worst perpetrators; they often make our lives extremely difficult. On the flip side, we have those beautiful people who come into our lives, and we are immediately drawn to them because of their beautiful radiating light that feels amazing just to be in their presence. These beings of light spread sparks of love and joy wherever they go. Their energy and light resonate with our own light within, within us, where our true authentic self exists, the self we strive to find, keep, and revel in. One of the most difficult life lessons we come here to learn, is the lesson of forgiveness. For to learn the art of forgiveness, you have to have someone or something to forgive. This means you have to experience something difficult (sometimes, extremely difficult) to receive the opportunity to forgive.

I will end with a Message from Love, entitled "The Art of Forgiveness."

# The Art of Forgiveness

"Everything is an opportunity, an opportunity to love and forgive or an opportunity to learn lessons that give you an opportunity to love and forgive. Ultimately, we are here to learn unconditional love and forgiveness. You all do this in your own unique way, with your own unique collection of players in this game called life. The ultimate goal is the same for every human being on earth. The quicker you understand this concept, the quicker your life becomes harmoniously filled with my flow of all that is Go(o)d. I fill you with the divine light of beauty and joy. Your perspective, the lens you view life with, is cleared. The veil is lifted. Suddenly, your eyes see with your heart rather than your unconscious mind, or ego. Forgiveness gives you freedom, freedom from the heavy chains that carry the burden of revenge, resentment, hatred, and sadness, keeping you in the dark."

"When you forgive someone who has made a transgression against you, you free yourself from the confines of the dark and negative ego energy that permeates your body. Realize instead that we are all here to teach each other. The one you need to forgive is often your biggest teacher. For how could you learn the art of forgiveness if you don't have the opportunity to forgive? With that said, the one who has done the transgression has to live with the heavy feeling of doing something that has hurt another. Their opportunity is to be accountable and ask for forgiveness, not only from you but also from themselves. This is the only way their souls can be set free."

"There's an opportunity for significant spiritual growth to take place on both ends in these situations. Everything in life that happens can be looked at in two ways, with love and forgiveness, or with fear and hatred. When you choose the path of love and forgiveness, you set yourself free. This doesn't mean that you have to agree with what was done to you; it just means you understand that no one is perfect. We are all here to learn, grow, and help each other. So let go, open your heart, and understand that people do what they do for their own reasons, for where they are on the continuum journey, from A to Z, striving for God consciousness."

"We come into and out of each other's lives for a reason, a season, or a lifetime for the ultimate purpose of growing spiritually, experientially. So take the lesson at hand, learn from it, forgive it, and let it go. You'll be lighter and happier for it in the end. As with everything and anything, my children, always remember, it's all good. Everything is always Go(o)d; it's what you choose to do with it that counts. Choose love."

# CHAPTER 5

## EPISODE 5

## Our Bubble World

I would like to talk about the world we live in today and the opportunity we have in these difficult times to create our own world within the world. We have a choice in whether to buy into the dark, heavy, negative energy of ego or to keep the lens we view the world with in a positive light. We are in control of it, even though it may seem as if we are not. I like to call our own personal world our bubble world.

I remember being at Disneyland a few years ago with my family. At 9 p.m., they close down Main Street to create one of the most magical experiences I've ever had. We were standing toward the back of the street, which gave us a full view of the entire show. There were people everywhere from all walks of life, waiting for this experience to begin. Over the loudspeaker, the narrator began telling a story; shortly thereafter, the beautiful voice of a princess began radiating an angelic song that seemed to bounce freely into the night air. The fireworks show began in the background, bursting sparks of light everywhere. It created an amazing feeling of overwhelming joy; resonating within was a feeling that seemed to light up my insides.

I glanced over my shoulder at this moment and saw a street vendor selling his goods. His cart was a continuous bubble machine. In the midst of this magical atmosphere, there were bubbles flying everywhere, into the night. I knew in this moment that I would never forget the feeling this experience created inside of me. I started watching the bubbles drift into the night air, some flying on their own, some in clusters and yet some coming together in pairs, breaking off and floating into the heavens. As I looked around at all the different folks standing with their own family and friends, I had this vision of everyone living in their own bubble world. I envisioned everyone's bubble coming in and out of each other's lives, sometimes for a moment and other times for a lifetime.

I thought about the fact that everyone's world was different and of their own making. Within our collective world and community, we all have our own world within the world. Further, we can create our personal world to be anything and everything we choose. Sometimes, we feel out of control in society, but in truth, we can create and control our own space. It is our choice to reflect a positive, loving, and harmonious atmosphere or a negative, dark, and heavy atmosphere. It is a reflection of your inner self.

What you feel gets reflected out and creates your landscape, the landscape of your personal world. Create your world to be that which you are and that which you want it to be, all by the choices you make in life. It's like a racquetball court; what you put out keeps hitting the wall and bouncing right back to you. If you want your life to be filled with the fullness of love, kindness, joy, and beauty, be what you wish it to be. The same will be created if you are choosing to live in fear, darkness, anger, and negativity. This, then, is what you will experience.

Everyone's bubble is floating around. Some connect in groups, some in pairs, and some remain solo. Some will stay connected for a lifetime and dissipate into the heavens together, where others will come in and out on their own path. Some are healthy and positive, yet others negative and toxic. There will also be those who tend to float along in their own little world, never thinking too much about anything or anybody, just floating through. All is exactly on time and on purpose. We teach each other through our differences, just as it is supposed to be. How else could we learn that which we are not? We are seeing the result of many dysfunctional bubbles in our collective world today. The hate, anger, and violence are the direct result of ego creating unhealthy bubble worlds that people live in. I encourage each and every one of you to create a beautiful, loving, and positive climate in your personal space and then observe how life reflects it back to you.

We all have a choice, and the road to ecstasy is yours for the choosing. Choose love and joy every time. When confronted with a choice, one will always feel better than the other. Choose the one that makes your whole body breathe a sigh of relief. Use your gifted barometer within to guide you along your way. Get to know it; pay attention to it. Learn what it feels like to make a choice that feels good and flows, and then the opposite choice that makes your gut wrench and keeps you stuck. This choice will feel like a roadblock that you keep running into, over and over again.

Once you start making choices that are congruent to your soul purpose, your life takes on a rhythm and flows like beautiful music, resonating within your heart. Your heart is truly where you will feel the harmony that tells you you're moving in the right direction. You will be creating your own heaven on earth. We all have the desire to live on earth as we do in the heavenly realm. Your soul remembers the feeling and continuously yearns to feel it. As you move forward, making these good choices, your being, your body, fully relaxes into this experience called life, and your bubble is filled with love. As the love floods your insides, it then radiates out to all who come into your space. It is then that your mission is accomplished, resulting in a feeling of peace and beauty. This beauty gets reflected out and becomes contagious. We are then fit to proceed, set an example, teach, and give back, spreading the love and light that is our true inheritance from God. Understand the importance of remembering that we all learn in life at our own pace and in our own unique way. Honoring this diversity is a wonderful gift and a beautiful exchange, as we are all collectively tied as one in this journey called life.

I will end with a Message from Love, entitled "Reflection and Choices."

. . . . . . . . . . . . . . . . . . . . . . . . . . . . . . . . . . . . . . . . . . . . . . . . . . . . . . . . . . . . . .

# Reflection and Choices

"*Take the time for reflection in your life. Life is a compounded string of choices, consequences, and lessons. As you get older, there is beauty in the aging process, in the gathering of experiences. Experiences allow you to see the opportunity you've had to grow in your spiritual self. As you get older, hindsight is a gift. You can see more clearly that you've always had choices, and the choices you made led you in a certain direction. Please know, my child, that there really is no wrong choice, for every choice allows you the opportunity to experience a feeling, a feeling that either feels good or not. Eventually, as you get older, you're more aware and listen to your gut. This is how you learn to stay on track with your divine mission, your dharma. When you are in alignment, your life will have a beautiful flow.*"

"*The feeling this flow creates becomes all that you want to feel. It is then that you learn to choose more wisely, imbued with my wisdom.*"

"*Celebrate getting older and wiser, for the wiser you get, the more peaceful your life becomes. It becomes a time of literally resting in my glory. Stay tuned and connected, celebrate your journey, and enjoy the gift of hindsight that getting older brings. It's a special time in life if you can relax and allow yourself*" *to look back and appreciate your journey. Everything is a positive if you look at it, knowing that the choices and outcomes were always an opportunity for spiritual growth. And spiritual growth is your purpose for coming to experience life on earth. Enjoy the process; enjoy the journey."*

# CHAPTER 6

## EPISODE 6

# Difficulty, Grief, and Loss

People often ask why bad things happen to good people. I would like to start out by personally extending my true heartfelt love and appreciation for the pain you feel when experiencing tragedy in your life. I don't want to downplay the true difficulty in dealing with grief, loss, or victimization. There is no easy way to get through the healing process when tragedy strikes, but there is a perspective that will help you on your path to healing.

At this time here on earth, we are experiencing terrible and random acts of violence perpetrated upon innocent people. Mother Nature seems to be a bit unhappy, to say the least. And our political differences are creating a very unhealthy environment to live in. Some may ask, "If there is a God, how could he allow these terrible things to happen?" The simple answer to that question is free will and personal accountability.

As we wrote earlier, we are all here experiencing a diversity of lessons, but we've forgotten who we really are. The vibration on earth is entrenched by the very low, dark, and heavy energy of ego, which could be referred to as Satan's spell. We are all accountable and responsible for our own choices. Many folks like to point the finger at others. It's important to remember that we all have a choice in how to react to any situation in our lives. No matter what happens to us, we should remember that we are always connected to a Higher Power that can help us in every way needed. We also have a choice to stay in the dark illusion of ego. Your outcome and experience thereafter will be a reflection of which way you have chosen to go.

Some people come into this life with a heavier, dense vibration for the purpose of having the experience of what that feels like and the journey it creates. Some are born into family dynamics with parents of this darker energy, void of love, which cause beautiful little souls to put up a shield of defense for protection; this then creates their personal experience. For those of you who are born into a dysfunctional or toxic family dynamic, remember that you are inherently a perfect child of God, that your earthly parents are here, fighting their way out of the illusion as well. Forgive them, and choose for yourself to live a life following the path of love.

We come into this life with the exact circumstances we need to learn what it is we are here to learn. There are many types of experiences in the process of becoming. These experiences are necessary in the learning of all things. Remember, we are born into this life with our memory wiped clean and progress through on our predestined plan; we all have diverse experiences, often becoming confused and scattered, consumed in our false self, our ego self. We are ultimately looking to break through the darkness and remember we are pure light. Once we have awakened, our journey toward enlightenment begins. We are living in a day and time with much controversy in regards to what's deemed to be right and what's deemed to be wrong. It is more important than ever to follow your heart and stay connected to your divine guidance. It is a difficult time to reside on earth. Know that when connected to the divine, there is nothing, no thing to fear. Be a soldier of the light. Help your brothers and sisters in their awakening from the dream that seems so real but in reality is only a playground, so to speak, for higher learning.

May we continue on this journey together and get the word out that there is a place where we can go to find safety and peace, a space within that is our true identity found in our heart. It's a place of permanence and truth, where you rest in the arms of God.

I will end with a Message from Love, entitled "Why Do Bad Things Happen to Good People?"

# Why Do Bad Things Happen to Good People?

*"There is so much evil that permeates the world. There is also free will, the basis of life on planet earth. All my children come into this earthly experience*

*with individual lessons they are here to learn. I am only able to intercede when asked. With that said, I can tell you that my innocent children do not suffer when despicable acts of horror are imposed upon them. They come home to me instantly in the fullness they left. If they remain on earth to spend the rest of their life making sense of such tragic acts, there are lessons that are only learned through these difficult events. Pain and agony are present not only for the victims but also for their loved ones, who feel the effect because of their relationship with them. The loved ones left behind will grieve and experience in their own way the loss of their beloved."*

*"I cannot control the actions of those who are so deeply surrounded by the darkness of evil. But I am there to lift you up, extending my hand, reaching it out to you with the love and strength you'll need to get through such immensely difficult times. Jesus's life was the perfect example of this; we must learn the meaning behind his last words on the cross: "Forgive them for they know not what they do." These tragedies are the ultimate test and simultaneously the biggest opportunity to learn the true meaning behind these profound last words."*

*"People who are capable of such despicable acts are so deeply entrenched in the darkness of ego, Satan's spell, that they are blind. They punish themselves because they live without any love, kindness, compassion, happiness, or joy. Their world is dark and terrible; they fight every day in literal sickness. Please recognize that I am there for you as you work to achieve success in the lesson of forgiveness; you will be immensely blessed with freedom and love, which fill your entire being. You are freed from the chains of horror that bind the*

soul when you are unable to forgive. For the perpetrators, they reside in the darkness, times a million, within their souls, and this is their lesson. I am there for them if and always will be, when they choose to reach out."

"Try to not allow the behavior of others to impinge on the love and joy you experience in your life. Know that the karmic balance of this life takes care of itself automatically. Choose love, and be that which you wish to experience. Teach those who have not found me yet to know me in their hearts, in their souls, and in their lives. This is the best you, as an individual child of God, can do. Go out this day and spread joy, set yourself free, and know that I am with you every step of the way."

# CHAPTER 7

## EPISODE 7

# The Different Stages in Life, and Finding Our Dharma

We are all looking for a sense of purpose in our lives. When we are in tune and flowing along in life as we are supposed to, on track, in the groove, it feels good, and we have a sense of purpose. This feeling of purpose is aligned with our personal gifts, our dharma. When we are living our dharma, we feel joyful. Joy is the emotion we feel when we are in alignment with God. You may ask, "How do I know I am living on purpose?" The answer is, you will feel it. This feeling will create a sense of excitement within. Your stamina and energy level will increase. You may wake up earlier than usual, not requiring as much sleep because there is an enthusiasm that you haven't felt in a long time (or possibly ever). Joy is the emotion that tells you you're on track and doing what you are here to do.

This sense of purpose may change at different times in your life, as Wayne Dyer puts it, in the morning, afternoon, and evening of your life. If you have not watched Dyer's movie, *The Shift,* I highly recommend doing so. He talks about the fact that we are all born with our own personal purpose, and until we find it, we will feel a sense of dissatisfaction. There will always be a tugging within that something is missing. He goes on to explain that as we enter into this life, we come in as pure and innocent souls; our parents exclaim a big thank you to God and proceed to say, "We'll take it from here."

And so our journey begins and we live this life intrenched in a realm that may or may not match the high vibration we come in with. Our childhood and youth set the stage for the rest of our life. It is during this time period that we are shaped from our family dynamics and environment. We go through our schooling, experience friendships and relationships, and try to find our place in society. We have either been given love or have had a void there. We are starting to gain an awareness of how this is shaping our world thus far.

As we go forward, from our late twenties to around fifty, we move into the experiential portion of our lives. This is where we find ourselves, get married, and choose to have a family (or not); others may find that the single life suits them better. You start your climb on the ladder of success, hopefully choosing a career that fits your newfound interests. People often jump from one job to another, trying to find their way, which may create struggles and unrest.

You will experience many different types of relationships through your jobs, romance, family, and friends. These relationships help you to better understand yourself, which teaches you your likes and dislikes. This period in life generally comes with many ups and downs, which is exactly on time and on purpose for the growth of your soul. It can also be a very taxing time, which naturally sets the stage for the remaining third of your life, the winding-down period, where priorities change and hindsight becomes 20/20. You have hopefully gained much wisdom from your choices and experiences, and you understand the well-known phrase, "older and wiser." There is a history that you can use to reflect upon that changes the lens you see life and the world with. It is a beautiful time of reflection, leading to wisdom.

You are now ready to fine-tune your life based on your experiences up to this point. You start to contemplate what you've accomplished or what you could have done differently and start thinking about what you may want the rest of your life to look like. If you have kids, they are usually ready to embark on their own to find their own way. Retirement becomes your focus. You have a newfound opportunity to revert back with yourself as an individual again, rather than continuing your role as a parent or in your career.

With that said, I'm very aware that once a parent, always a parent. But typically, unless there are special circumstances that keep your children with you, it is a time to refocus on you. Nevertheless, life changes, and you are ready to change with it. The stage is set for the evening portion of your life to begin. I remember feeling like I was twenty years old again, trying to decide what to do with the rest of my life. You have the opportunity to reinvent yourself anew, utilizing all the wisdom you've gained thus far. You can reflect back on your life and see where there were times of sudden pivotal change, where disappointments led you in a new direction that turned out to be the perfect direction. Or maybe you found yourself dealing with difficult people who in the end totally changed your trajectory. Possibly you can see that a certain choice set in motion a direction that created a new perspective.

In the evening portion of life, you can see that your life has taken you on your own unique journey, showing you that there's more to life than meets the eye. There were pivotal times that created a change that was not the direction you intended to go but turned out to be exactly perfect: perfect in a positive way, but other times, perfectly difficult. You reflect back on times where the right person showed up to deliver the perfect message seemingly out of nowhere, which put you on the exact path you needed to go. This is universal guidance helping from the unseen divine realm, which is there awaiting your recognition and yearning for you to see their loving guidance in your life. This guidance has been there from the day you were born with your memory wiped clean, in order to experience life in the illusion of this earthly realm. Some call these instances coincidences, but I suggest there is no such thing as coincidence. They are synchronicities or divinely orchestrated miracles. It is the universe's way of helping us navigate through life. For what kind of loving Father would send us to this challenging task without help?

Certainly not our pure and unconditionally loving Father in heaven. So know and trust that we are all taken care of and watched over, always. As you learn to tune your ear and open your eyes to the language of the universe, you realize we are never alone. There are divine helpers waiting for you to recognize their presence in your life. They have been there all along, sometimes very apparent but other times waiting in the background as you make choices that teach you one thing or another.

Again I say, all is well; everything is perfect as long as we choose to see it that way. As our purpose in life shifts during the different stages we go through, remember that it will flow easier when we move in the direction we are meant to go. Use your barometer to know that you are where you are supposed to be at any given time on your journey. This concept will never steer you wrong, so stay tuned, and always be in touch with the way you feel.

I will end with a Message from Love, entitled "Free Will."

······················································································

# Free Will

*"I wait patiently at the threshold of your heart, waiting for you to find me within the likes of you, waiting for the moment that you ask for my divine*

love to be known within you. I give my children free will to make their own choices. All the while I sit back, waiting for you to choose me. When you are ready to choose a life with me, my response is immediate, but you may have to decipher it, for I speak to you in unconventional ways. Part of the journey with me is to learn the language I speak. This comes by how you feel. It may also come from a beautiful bird suddenly singing outside your window. It could be a stranger who delivers the perfect message or a song on the radio that sings you a beautiful lyric of love."

"Synchronicity is my doing. You may call it coincidence, but it is always a miracle, a gift that helps you know that I am with you, teaching you my language. This is how I am able to gift myself and my love to you. It allows you to grow your faith, which in turn draws you closer to me. This cycle is the ultimate way you start your walk on the yellow brick road with me. Follow the yellow brick road, and enjoy the journey of life along the way. Keep your eyes wide open to see and your ears clear to hear, for I am with you always, always, in ways that will be a joy to experience, ways that are filled with the grace that could only come from the Creator of all. The source of literally everything. Find me, feel me in all that you are, in all that you do, and in all that is. For my love is, all that is."

# CHAPTER 8

## EPISODE 8

# Relationships and Unconditional Love

When we realize that love is all there is, we have a consistent answer to every question in life: just love. When we learn that nothing else exists in any real way except love, then the way we look at life changes. When we change our perception to look at all people with eyes of love, we gain the gifts of compassion, forgiveness, nonjudgment, and humility. This perception helps us realize that fear, the ill actions of others, and illness in the body and mind are a result of the lack of awareness that love is all there is; it's the only thing that is real. Therefore, in all other instances, it is ego, reveling in its dark state of being, in fear or lack of love, creating a perception and a feeling of being unloved or unlovable.

If you find yourself feeling either of these two emotions, know that you are not in alignment with the source of everything, the universe, that is only abundant love. If you take this concept into your relationships in life, truly understand that the basis of happiness is to just love, your compassionate heart will kick in. If you learn to not take things personally but realize that another's acting out is a call for love, you'll change the dynamics in your relationships. When you unite with another, whether it's a friend, family member, or a romantic partner, you have your own mission you are here to accomplish.

In all these relationships, support each other's journey. Accept each other for who they are, at face value, and do not try to change them into who you'd like them to be. A healthy and good relationship always reflects this; it has continuous understanding and compassion for the other, based in love. As you support and love one another, the love between you becomes glorious. Glorious because it feels so good to truly love another so much that you honor their unique spiritual journey, which in turn helps you honor your own. The harmony that this brings within yourself and within your relationships will be the source of the love, peace, and joy that you seek.

Remember, it's always about the way things make you feel. Strive to always feel at peace and to give that peace to those in your immediate circle, as well as those who come into your space. This will not only feed you; it will also be your gift to any and all who have the pleasure of being around you, for what you give out is what you receive tenfold. It becomes a win-win for all. Even though we are all here living and walking on our own unique journey, the paradox is that we are all here interacting for the purpose of teaching each other lessons through these relationships. When your heart is in the right place, filled with love, kindness, and true compassion, you exude the beautiful trait of humility.

Humility is derived from a place within, where your soul kneels down in gratitude for the grace of God within. Ego is completely wiped out of your existence, and you are filled with pure love. Humility is a beautiful characteristic that shows your inner beauty and spiritual health. Humility does not brag or boast of achievements; the awareness is focused on gratitude for the blessings from the divine. Strive always to be the best you that you can be, in all areas of your life. Realize that your achievements are due to your innate and individual gifts from God. Seek to experience success, feeling grateful and blessed. For in this way, the outcome will portray itself with the beautiful trait of humility. Humility loves, forgives, and has no judgment. It merely seeks its pleasure by radiating peace.

When you are blessed to be in the company of someone who radiates peace derived from humility, you glimpse a view of residing in the divine realm with God. It truly is a divine trait and so very pleasurable to be around. Jesus was an example of pure humility. Gentle and serene in his mannerisms, he was a beautiful reflection of divine perfection. As ego is edged out of your being, humility naturally replaces it. Use this as a personal barometer as you continue on your journey back to the divine. Know that when you seek the love of God, your heart will be softened, and humility will fill your soul. Ultimately, peace will be felt not only by you but by all who will be blessed to be in your space; consequently, your relationships will be harmonious.

Never forget that all relationships are perfectly orchestrated destiny; you have come together for a predestined purpose. If you look at your relationships in this way, with eyes of love, it will set your soul free, void of turmoil and frustration. Soar with freedom and love in your life, truly acknowledging and honoring your own journey as well as your journey with others, knowing that your connection is on time and on purpose for the growth of your soul. Life will automatically reward your hard work with love, peace, and kindness within yourself and within your relationships.

I will end with a Message from Love, entitled "Tolerance and Diversity."

- - - - - - - - - - - - - - - - - - - - - - - - - - - - - - - - - - - - - - - - - - - - - - - - - - - - - - - - - - - - -

# Diversity and Tolerance

*"My child, this day and every day, move forward in life with the confidence you need to stand tall in who you are. Stand tall, for in this world, there will be much controversy. Some controversial conversations unite, and others separate. Honor the goodness this diversity brings in your different relationships. Through this diversity, you learn tolerance and understand the many pathways that lead to the ultimate goal of loving each other unconditionally, the same way that I, your Father in heaven, love each and every one of my children. Your journey is my journey, and the experience there is for the good of all. We are here to teach*

each other through how we feel when we interact with each other. Chemistry is created, not only for romantic purposes, but also on a platonic level, so you can engage in relationships that are more than just an acquaintance."

"This is where the majority of life lessons are learned. You learn the many ways of experiencing all types of love, ultimately striving to find pure and unconditional love, a love that not only binds the two of you together, but the two of you with me. This is the ultimate love that all my children on earth are yearning for in their hearts and souls. It may not even be acknowledged, but your soul knows and remembers that this is the piece that is missing."

"When it is found, it brings satisfaction and peace, like a coming home, and you finally feel fulfilled. There is a sense that your mission on earth is complete, and now it's time to just dance and enjoy the experience of the beautiful exchange of truly loving with no expectations, no strings attached, allowing each other to truly be who you are here to be. Honoring the differences encourages each other's spiritual growth and fully engages in the beautiful love that can only be felt in this sacred union. You will know these people immediately, for there is a feeling of knowing them before. In a romantic relationship, you will melt into each other's arms as one, breathe as one, and feel a deep sigh of relief, for you will feel a sense of completion and contentment that you've never quite felt before. This, my love, is how you'll know that you have found the one. And remember, "the one" has a twofold meaning: you with your beloved, which in turn is you with me."

# CHAPTER 9

## EPISODE 9

### Compassion

Life tends to roll along with its many ups and downs, failures and achievements, elation and grief, happy times and sadness. It ebbs and flows, creating experiences that become the story of our life. We feel elation when it's on a high and a heaviness when times get tough. Struggles in life feel real, and yet they are really an illusion of the earthly realm. If we remember to always maintain the perspective that everything happens for a reason and is on time and on purpose, it helps us keep a positive outlook, even in the difficult times. It would also behoove us to remember that struggles are all relative, meaning my struggles may not seem as insurmountable as yours and vice versa, but nevertheless, for each individually, they are real and are one's own true set of circumstances. It is important to never compare. You cannot truly understand what another is going through, unless you've walked in their shoes. Strive to never judge and to never compare. Know that what is true and real for you is just that, and the same goes for your fellow human being. I use the term "human being" on purpose because struggles are a human emotion. The truth is, there are no struggles unless we choose to make them struggles because again, everything is perfect just the way it is.

I do not want to discount the fact that we all have difficulties and feel unsettled from time to time; after all, we are having this human experience and no matter how enlightened we strive to be, we are still living in this very dense illusion on this earth plain, and sometimes, it's hard to see the forest from the trees. Try as you may, try as you might to be positive, but sometimes, confusion and turmoil set in. As long as you remember and understand what the basis of that is, the illusion, and you have learned the truth that all is well always, you will move forward, grow spiritually, and see the light at the end of the tunnel.

Strive to always look through the fog and find the silver lining in the clouds. Do yourself a big favor by not trying to keep up with the Joneses, for their lessons and destiny are not yours, and yours are not theirs. Never compare your circumstances with theirs, for it will always bring you down. In addition, do not impose your ideals on them. View life with these eyes, and a beautiful understanding naturally takes place and creates peace within, as well as in your relationships. Live your life with this awareness and perspective, and you will save yourself a lot of strife along the way.

The goal is to always do you and appreciate others and have compassion for those doing the same, for isn't this exactly what you desire for yourself from others? Which segues beautifully into the Golden Rule: "Do unto others as you would have them do unto you." If we could all live life from this simple but profound principle, always acting in accordance to treating others the way we would like to be treated, actually taking a moment before acting and reacting, to think about this kind and compassionate concept, there would be a lot less strife and conflict in our lives and consequently in the world.

Remember that everyone's perspective, the lens they see the world and people with, comes from their own experiences. It may have been tainted by a past filled with dysfunctional behavior, either imposed upon them or them imposing it on others, or enriched with an abundance of beautiful and loving goodness; very often, it's a combination of both. This lends perspective to how we view life. Whether it's a positive or a negative, we have a choice to make it what we want it to be at any given moment.

For a moment, dream about the exact circumstances you want your life to look like. Actually play the part of the you that you would like to be. Feel the way it feels in your story, your movie that you are producing. See it in your mind's eye. Sit with it; enjoy the feeling of being what you dream to be. Watch this movie daily, and see how you literally manifest this life to come into existence. The key is to believe. Believe it into reality, even if it seems impossible; remember, there is an unseen divine realm and force that is ignited when you practice this daily. A few years ago, I was in a very magical and synchronistic time period in my life. It was so exciting every day to wake up and look forward to what magical experience I was going have that day. I wrote a poem during that time that encompasses this concept; it goes like this:

Bow your head and know.

Open your arms and trust.

Send a magnetic cord from your heart into the universe,

filled with all your hopes, dreams, and desires.

It will combust into a million pieces, like fireworks filled

with magic.

The magical universe will take it from there.

And then, just surrender.

Life is magical for those with eyes to see and ears to hear. Learn the language of the universe, for it is constantly speaking to you. Tap in and notice; pay attention and connect with this magical divine force that is there to co-create a beautiful life with you and for you. Enjoy and share in the glorious light and love that living with this perspective brings. Consequently, the lens you see life with changes into a beautiful creation of love for not only yourself but for all things and all people.

And this is how we change the world. We as individual human beings can make a difference, but the difference starts with you.

I will end with a Message from Love, entitled "Intention."

. . . . . . . . . . . . . . . . . . . . . . . . . . . . . . . . . . . . . . . . . . . . . . . . . . . . . . . . . . . . . . . . .

## Intention

*"Set your intention upon whatever it is you desire. Know beyond a shadow of a doubt that it will come into fruition. By means of the law of attraction, it will. The key to success is pure and genuine intention that truly comes from the heart, a trust that is unwavering, and the knowledge that it will. You are built with this ability within the network of your soul; everybody is capable of directing their lives in the direction they wish it to go. It takes much practice and training in the heart, soul, and mind to stay positive. Stay true, and trust that your desires come from a place within that is connected with your highest good. You can and will truly manifest what you want and need in your life, if you can dream it, visualize it, and send it out into the universe. Then, "poof," let it go. Trust in God's divine timing, and allow it to come to pass. Patience is a virtue. Keep your intention set with this knowing, and watch it unfold."*

*"In the meantime, be the best that you can be; give love, receive love, and be what you want, and in return, life will invariably take care of you, always. So sit back and enjoy the ride, for the longing is a part of the journey."*

# CHAPTER 10

## EPISODE 10

# Balance and Moderation

Balance is the key to a beautiful life. We've all heard the saying, "Moderation in all things." Balance and moderation provides the key to maintaining a peaceful, loving, and happy life. It is also the key to a beautiful body, mind, and soul. It is imperative for good health physically as well as mentally. Extremes and excess create imbalance and stagnation. Both are just as destructive, resulting in unhappiness. "A little bit of this, a little bit of that" and "Work hard, play hard" are good mottos to live by. Too much one way or another, without the balance, can create addiction, result in obsessions, and cloud your vision.

Your body, mind, and soul resonate with balance, and consequently, your life flourishes in this environment. You can create balance in your life through the choices you make; harmony is the result. Your health is directly affected by the balance or imbalance in life. If you are out of alignment long enough, your body tries to signal you through how you feel. If you pay attention and understand this concept, you can catch it early and make the changes that need to be made in order to rebalance it. If you choose not to pay attention, your body may manifest illness. The longer you ignore its alarm, the deeper the illness becomes. I personally believe this is the root of illness in your body. It stems from your emotional health. Your body responds to love; as a matter of fact, it is love.

As we mentioned before, love is all there is, and love heals everything. This is why it's so important to take care of yourself. Showing self-love and taking time for you is not selfish; it's imperative for a beautiful, healthy, and wonderful life. It is in the giving to yourself that you are able to maintain a strong and healthy body, the temple that houses your soul. This attention feeds and nourishes your body, mind, and soul. It is in the nurturing of self that you get filled up so that you have something to give back. This is reciprocity at its best. If you are filled up and healthy, you are more apt to give to others. If your tank is depleted, you have nothing to give.

This is an important concept, especially for mothers. Women have a tendency to be givers. It's a natural part of a woman's feminine nature. They attend to their family and often do not make time for themselves. This is known as the Superwoman syndrome. I would like to encourage mothers in particular to realize the importance of taking time to fill your cup so you can maintain the strength that it takes to care for your family.

All husbands should encourage their wives to do this on a regular basis. I would also encourage married couples to take time to nourish their relationship as well. Date nights keep the spark going, which is necessary for connection.

Strive to create a balanced and healthy environment for the whole family. It's really not a luxury; it's imperative for the success of the family unit as a whole. Creating a beautiful life also filters into your home environment. Create a home that resonates with who you are. Fill it with objects that feel good and represent things you love. Fill it with a decor that has meaning to you, your partner, and others in your family.

Every time you walk through the door, you should breathe a sigh of relief that you are home in your personal sanctuary. Keep it clean and free of clutter. Your insides are affected by your environment. I'm sure you've entered a place and immediately felt like you couldn't get out of there soon enough. Conversely, after entering an environment where it totally resonates and you can't seem to get enough, it feels amazing. There is a feeling and an energy that is created with different people, places, and things. Take note and be aware of this concept in your personal world. Create your home to be a sanctuary for you and your family. Take pride in keeping it neat and clean. Teach your children the importance of creating a beautiful home environment. It will directly affect the dynamic in the home. If it is beautiful and well maintained, you will feel peaceful. If it is cluttered and dirty, it will feel chaotic. The size of your home doesn't matter. It has everything to do with making what you have unique to you. Keep it up with pride and pleasure.

This concept should be a theme for all things and people in your life. When you take the time to pay attention to the detail with love, the detail pays attention to you with the same love that you give. This is the natural phenomenon of reciprocity at work. What you put out you get in return. This goes for everyone and everything in your life. Do not allow yourself to make excuses about not having enough time or energy. Make it a priority. You will reap the rewards for making it important by enjoying a loving, peaceful and beautiful life in all areas. Give this gift to yourself and your family. The result will be worthwhile.

I will end with a Message from Love entitled "Balance and Your Own Personal Space."

· · · · · · · · · · · · · · · · · · · · · · · · · · · · · · · · · · · · · · · · · · · · · · · · · · · · · · · · · · · · · · · · · · · · · · · · · ·

# Balance and Your Own Personal Space

"The objects that people keep in their home define who they are."

"Take a look around your home; notice the way it feels. Is it neat and tidy, or is it cluttered? Are there piles of excess, or is it open and spacious? Have you intentionally placed things in your home that have purpose and meaning? When you walk in the door, do you breathe a sigh of relief?"

"Your home is your sanctuary, your own little world within the world. It should be your place of retreat from the busy and chaotic outside world. It *should be your place of rejuvenation. It is directly reflective of your inner state of mind. If you are feeling heavy, bogged down, and overwhelmed, your home environment will often reflect the same. This is why it feels so good to purge or do spring-cleaning. As you purge any clutter and excess from your home, you will naturally feel a sense of freedom and peace. The things you choose to decorate your home with should reflect who you are as a person. Be intentional with what you choose to bring into your environment. Create your home to be your sacred space, a place where you completely resonate. It should give you a big sigh of relief to walk through your door and say, "Ah, yes, I am home." The size of your home or apartment doesn't matter, only that is feels Go(o)d."*

*"This will look different for everyone of my children because you are all unique in your own way. Take the time to figure out for yourself what makes you feel peaceful and at ease. Go with that, and put heart and good intention in as you arrange, decorate, and fill your personal space with that which makes you feel beautiful within. Keeping your space clean and uncluttered will allow you to feel this inside yourself. It creates an environment and an energy that vibrates at a higher level. In turn, it raises your own vibration within. This becomes a win/win. It will reflect on your physical and emotional health as well as your state of mind."*

*"Take some time to walk around your home and assess what it feels like. Put love, intention, and dedication into this process, and feel the difference in what it brings. Remember that balance is one of the most important keys to a life well lived, a life that can truly be enjoyed. Balance and moderation will lend itself to happiness. Everyone is searching for happiness. Happiness is*

*derived from the feeling of joy. And joy, my children, is of me. So keep me close, and watch your life unfold in a way that will surely be joy-filled."*

*"As you create beauty, balance, and moderation, your body responds with joy. This beautiful response creates an overall feeling of well-being. As you continue living your life in this way, you suddenly realize that this is key to living a life that is full of delight. Oh, and by the way, delight is also of me. So carry on living, laughing, and enjoying a life that is full, full of all that is wonderful, beautiful, and lovely. All of which are of me."*

# CHAPTER 11

## EPISODE 11

# Responsibility and Respect

"If you can't say anything nice, don't say anything at all" is another profound motto to live by. To keep your life surrounded and moving in a positive direction, it's important to be mindful of the words you choose to speak; in addition, be aware of the words spoken to you. There's an invisible energy that words carry. This energy is always felt by both parties participating in a conversation. They will either be felt in a light and positive way or a negative and heavy way. Both parties in a conversation will be affected by the climate that's created. Even if you are imposing the negativity, you will walk away feeling heavy, as will the other person. The same occurs in the opposite situation; if positivity is shared, it is felt through an ease and creates a peaceful experience. Everyone should always walk away from time spent together feeling good and uplifted. Otherwise, why would you choose to participate?

Having boundaries with the people, places, and things in your life can be a challenging life lesson, but it's of utmost importance in the pursuit of a happy life. The word *no* can be so uncomfortable to speak; people often compromise their own well-being for the sake of not rocking the boat. Being afraid of hurting another's feelings or never wanting to put someone out can lead to an awkward and unhealthy outcome. There is an empowering feeling that gets created within when you choose to stand in your truth. The truth is, you have a responsibility to stand up for yourself in this life. It is not a selfish act to take care of you; in fact, it's your responsibility. If you don't take care of yourself, no one else will, and it really is no one else's responsibility to do so.

It feels good when you learn how to say no. Your body responds in a way that feels liberating and self-empowering (self-empowering in the most humble way, not in an ego power way). You cannot control the actions and choices of others, but you can control your responses and decisions. Unfortunately, children have no choice when born into a dysfunctional family dynamic, but they do have a choice in how they handle it once they are old enough to change the trajectory of their own life. Again, a very difficult life lesson, to say the least, but realizing they are in control of their destiny at some point in their life is very liberating.

When difficulties arise in relationships of all types, I believe that everything can be healed and worked out through conversation. A mature conversation allows both parties to speak their truth and then listen with no judgment. Preferably this is done directly with the individual; if that isn't possible, a trusted friend or professional. Most importantly, never hold it in and allow it to fester; this is how disease (dis-ease) begins. Get to the bottom of an issue, either by coming to an understanding or deciding to just agree to disagree. There are always two sides to every story. Remember that everyone views life through the eyes of their own personal journey; it's okay to disagree with another's outlook or opinion. That is healthy. It's not okay, however, to impose your view on another and insist on being right. Diversity is what makes the world go round. Respect, understanding, and kindness is the goal in any dispute. Kindness always prevails, leading to a happy and positive result for all involved. Choose to resolve disputes and allow them to dissipate into dust. This is a responsible choice, and making responsible choices filters into many areas of life.

The goal is living with good intention, morals, and values, creating happiness, which consequently creates joy. Hanging onto anything negative negates a positive outcome. Let's talk for a moment about responsible choice in other areas in life. For example, paying your bills. If you are living in mainstream society, you have reoccurring bills to pay each month to keep afloat. When you choose to pay your bills first and then use the leftover money for pleasure, you are creating a foundation in your life of security and peace. Conversely, if you choose to use your earnings first for pleasure and secondly to pay your bills, you have made an irresponsible choice that compounds each month to set in motion a foundation of insecurity, chaos, and turmoil. The excitement derived from a moment of pleasure will never compare to the security and peace of mind created by making a responsible choice.

This is just one example, but there are many areas in your life where this concept plays out the same. The consequences for choosing instant gratification will always be short-lived, and you will be left with the residual heaviness that choosing irresponsibly creates. Reality and responsibilities are a constant and do not go away. If you choose to take care of the responsibilities in your life first, you create a flow; you tap into divine magic and will find that somehow, someway, you still have enough for the pleasure. The mere fact that you do not carry the heaviness and stress from making an irresponsible choice creates pleasure and ease, which lends itself to the flow.

Strive in all that you do and all decisions that you make to be mindful and tap into the flow. We've all heard the saying "Go with the flow." Trust that if you take care of your life, life will take care of you. Understand that the word *life* is synonymous with God and that going with the flow is God in motion in your life. Allow God to work his magic and miracles, resulting in the comfort of an innate knowledge that all is well. No matter which way things go in life, together with your good intention and God's divine timing, all is well and divinely orchestrated, always.

I wrote a prayer during a period in my life where letting go seemed to be a reoccurring theme. I would like to share it with you.

It is a good one to have in your back pocket, so to speak, for whenever you are presented with a situation that feels out of your control. Sometimes, you just need to be reminded that there's a divine force that is always there at your beck and call to help lead the way. The prayer goes like this:

And so I lay, completely open and vulnerable to your way, my Father. I surrender to you with fullness in my heart and watch as your guidance fulfills my dreams. In love with love, a hopeless romantic, an eternal optimist, I move forward without fear and live in the courage and strength that our bond creates. Your miracles exceed beyond expectation, and my life feels complete. Thank you for your love, guidance, and direction on my journey to becoming whole and the fulfilling of my dreams and life purpose. Amen.

I will end with a Message from Love, entitled "No Expectations."

## No Expectations

I have no expectations. I'm totally in your hands.
Whatever you want to do with me is fine.
–Quote from Wayne Dyer's movie, *The Shift*

*"As you awaken each and every morning, open your eyes and greet the new day with the absolute glory of the feeling of me within you. Take the time to commune and be aware of the beautiful peace and love that fill your heart and*

*body with each breath you take. Set this feeling in motion by giving yourself permission to let go and allow my hand to lead and guide your day. Expect the unexpected in the most beautiful ways possible. For truly, my children, when you follow my lead by being in tune with your feelings within, you will experience a life lived, literally, in my glory. When you live day by day, in tune with the divine that surrounds you, you live in a magical world. This happens when you completely let go of control and give in to trust, trusting that there is more going on in this life than meets the eye, knowing that within, there is something bigger guiding your every thought and move. Ultimately, you move through your daily experience with complete love, kindness, compassion, peace, and joy within your heart, not only for yourself but for everyone who crosses your path. When you can fully achieve this on a daily basis, your life will reflect this back to you, and you will be existing in this world but not necessarily of it. So let go and allow my hand, the hand of God, to guide your every thought, your every move, and watch how your life changes in the most beautiful ways."*

# CHAPTER 12

## EPISODE 12

# Divine Helpers

I believe that an invisible realm exists simultaneously with us here in the realm that we can see. I believe that we are all born into this life with our own personal guardian angel, who is assigned to us for guidance and protection throughout our lifetime. I also believe that sometimes, we have a whole team of divine helpers, and other times, not as many, depending on our needs and personal lessons that we are here to experience. I like to refer to this team as our own personal divine posse. If you take the time to develop a relationship with them, you'll see that they are speaking to us all the time; we just have to learn their language. In times of emergency or urgent need, we may actually hear their voice (typically, in my experience, a voice right outside your ear). They may also speak to you telepathically by infusing ideas within your mind; you may feel goosebumps. At other times, they may even step in and take over for a moment to prevent a harmful or dangerous situation.

Many authors have written beautiful accounts of their direct experiences with these angelic helpers. They teach you how to develop a personal relationship with these beautiful divine beings. Some people are gifted with the sight to actually see them. I read a beautiful article, an excerpt from one of Lorna Byrne's many insightful books, where she claims that she has never seen anyone on this earth who did not have an angel with them at all times. There are also numerous accounts of near-death experiences (NDEs) where people return to their human life to give us a beautiful description of the angels and divine beings on the other side, who are readily awaiting us when we transition. I would highly recommend reading books on this subject, for they can help us navigate through this life. Anita Moorjani wrote a book called *Dying To Be Me*, which is her incredible story of being on her death bed with stage 4 cancer, having a NDE, and returning to completely heal and recount the profound experience and words of wisdom she learned on the other side.

I believe that some people, known as psychics and mediums, have come into this life with a special gift; their intuitive sense is highly developed. They are here, as messengers, to give us the help and guidance we could all use from time to time. Mediums are blessed with the ability to connect with our loved ones who have passed over and give us messages directly from them. I have learned that our loved ones just want us to know they are okay and that they are still with us in spirit. I also believe that a group of human beings began coming to the earth in the early 1990s to aid in the spiritual awakening.

These individuals may be referred to as lightworkers or old souls. Their sole purpose in this life is to help usher in the new age of spirituality, helping folks stretch beyond the box of strict religious dogma and open their hearts and minds to a philosophy that creates unity instead of separation and superiority. Similarly, there is the newest generation of kids, called the crystal children. These children are highly intuitive and enter at a very high vibration. Both lightworkers and crystal children have a natural and innate connection to the divine realm. We come into this life with many ways to connect to this invisible realm beyond the thin gossamer veil. We all have the ability to develop a relationship with these angelic beings. It starts with a desire and an open mind to take the initiative to delve into the unknown. You need an openness and desire to believe in something purely on faith. There are so many wonderful ways to start this journey. Reach out and be cognizant of the messages and synchronicities that lead you in new directions. Ask for guidance from the realm beyond your sight. Take advantage of all the movies, documentaries, books, and recordings that have been written and produced on these subjects. Refer often to the list in chapter 13, offering twenty-six ways to live a beautiful and peaceful life. Then watch how your life unfolds to the mystery and magic that living with the desire to be open and have faith in the unknown brings.

When you tap into the magic of universal guidance, you realize that there is no such thing as coincidence. It is really serendipity or synchronicity. Our lives are full of divinely orchestrated miracles that occur on a daily basis. By learning the language of the universe, you become a part of the beautiful and magical way that you are led down the destined path of your life: the thought that pops into your head out of nowhere, the opportunity that comes up at the perfect time, the perfect message in a song on the radio or TV at the precise moment you turn it on, the random stranger who says the right thing at just the right time, your loved ones who call just as you were thinking of them, the bumper sticker or license plate on the car that validates what you are thinking right as it comes into your view. We are surrounded by a host of divine helpers, universally as well as personally, and they are constantly speaking to us. Our job individually is to tune in and learn the language these universal beings speak. Accidents typically are no accident; they usually carry a message. Our homes and vehicles are infused with our personal energy, which will often carry various messages that help guide and direct our lives. Pay attention to the subtle and repetitive ways that try to get your attention; if ignored, these messages become louder, stronger, and more profound. Learn to decipher the code. Make metaphors out of what may be passed off as an accident or a tragedy; it's usually trying to tell you something. Dig deep, contemplate, and try to figure it out (just know that you are never alone).

Again, we come into this life with our own personal angels and guides. We gain more guidance at times of need and float along with only a few at other times. But what is certain is that we are always taken care of; we are always guided and protected, especially during times of strife or danger. Remember that we are here in this life with free will, so realize that most of the time, they will sit back and wait to be asked for their help. They cannot interfere with your choices, but they will protect you when needed and intercede when asked. As with God, these divine helpers will show themselves through serendipitous and synchronistic ways. Learn how you are being helped and guided, learn the language in which the divine universal energy speaks to you, and always give thanks. It promises to be amazing, fulfilling, and awe-inspiring to live your life basking in the miracles and magic of the divine and knowing that you are never alone.

I will end with a Message from Love, entitled "Ask and Ye Shall Receive."

## Ask and Ye Shall Receive

*"Ask and ye shall receive; but the way that you shall receive will not be in a conventional way. So think outside the box because the way I answer your prayer will never be how you think I will. So learn, my children, to expand your minds so you can decipher my ways of teaching. This is so you will always know that it could only come from me, your Father in heaven, and my array of divine helpers. I have many helpers who come in many forms; take the time to connect and create a personal relationship with them. They are all awaiting*

*your attention and acknowledgment. My children are all surrounded by their own personal group of divine helpers. It is a promise and a gift that I have given to each and every one of you who has chosen to live on planet earth. This lifetime for most of you is filled with many lessons, some harder and more tragic than others. Know that whatever you are experiencing is exactly on time and always on purpose for whatever was decided prior to you coming into this life here on earth. You have all agreed on the comings and goings of your interactions with each other."*

*"If you feel a special bond with someone, it is there for you to recognize and have the gift of remembering each other in your hearts. This creates special and wonderful relationships. Likewise, those you may be resistant to are there for a reason. Listen to your feelings, and be cautious of creating relationships with these folks. They come into your life for the opportunity to learn and experience your intuitive sixth sense. Learn to listen to your gut, your barometer that is gifted to you to help you stay on the path."*

*"All these things, my loves, are part of the journey you have agreed to go on, for many different reasons. Some for personal growth, and others to assist others, helping them on their own personal journey of growth and awakening. Other times, it's for karmic purposes, and sometimes to just plainly experience life as a spiritual being in a human body. We interact for all these reasons; we come into and out of each other's lives, exactly on time and on purpose, for the growth and experience of all, ultimately leading you to you find me in your hearts and in your souls and in your lives. I love all my children the same and understand their purpose and journey. Please always know that there truly is*

*no judgment on my part with you. For what unconditionally loving Father would have judgment on his children when he understands everything they are trying to accomplish? Doing this with amnesia and living in an earth school is so very dense and difficult to navigate through."*

*"All is always well, my children. All I ask is that you truly do the best you can with the limitations and tools you are born with. The rest is just a journey of love and forgiveness, ultimately finding me within your heart. You are my shining stars. So go out and live your life to the fullest, dropping fragments of love everywhere you go, every step you take. Teach my Word to your fellow brothers and sisters so they too may feel my love within. Don't try to figure life out. It's not meant to be deciphered; it's meant to be lived in the here and now, as an adventure, one day at a time, one moment at a time. Wake each morning in awe and excitement for what the new day may bring. Give thanks to the beauty and freedom that are bestowed upon you. Rejoice in the here and now and just love. Love life, love people, love experiencing what the new day brings. You are my light and my love; through all of my children, I bask in experiencing life through you, the you of me united as one. So go enjoy this day with eyes wide open and ears clear to hear the language of the universe, which pours out of your very soul and surrounds you every moment of every day."*

# CHAPTER 13

## EPISODE 13

## Living a Harmonious Life in the Magic

Living in the magic and living in the flow is like a bird's angelic voice singing in the morning air. The peace that is felt at the dawning of each new day is so beautifully calming. The joy that you experience when surrounded by those you love is priceless. The sense of awe when communing in nature is inspiring. The amazing feeling that is reciprocated when being in service to another fills your soul. The connection to the divine that our soul feels when in a state of gratitude creates wholeness. The longing we all feel to find and meld into the one is eternal. The chills we get all over when the truth has been spoken is a miracle. The zing of an aha moment sets us free. The relief of finding your voice and speaking your truth creates strength. The courage of moving outside the box and out of your comfort zone initiates success. The beauty of forgiveness creates unconditional love. The honoring of diversity breeds nonjudgment. And the delight in experiencing children reminds us of our innocence.

This is what life looks like when we are filled with and living in God's grace. We have a choice on how we decide to live this life we are given in this earth school. We can create anything we want just by our perception of it. Change your thoughts to change your life. It all boils down to a choice. Choose love or choose fear. Love is God, and fear is ego. The second we choose God, we receive his grace, his gift to all who find him within.

I will leave you now with twenty-six (no particular reason for that number but just the way they flowed out) beautiful ways to live life to the fullest. These steps will lead you on an extraordinary adventure, culminating in abundance and a life filled with happiness and joy. You then proceed to exude this happiness and joy, which becomes obvious to all who are gifted to be your space. As this cycle continues, the world becomes a better place with every step and breath you take.

1. No matter where or how you are born into this life, be it a positive or negative situation, know that you have everything you need within your own capabilities to make the life you dream of. Be brave, trudge forward, work hard, be kind, and dream it into fruition.

2.  Practice the Golden Rule: Do unto others as you would have them do unto you. Never judge your brothers or sisters, for you don't know where they've been, what their life purpose is, or what lessons they are here to experience on their own personal path. Everyone is always doing the best they can with what they have to work with and where they are on the continuum of moving through life toward awakening and enlightenment.

3.  In all your relationships, be loving, kind, and understanding. Do not try to change another, and do not strive to always be right. Instead, appreciate each other's differences and views. Be open.

4.  Be honest and trustworthy, for you cannot have a healthy relationship otherwise. Trust is hard to gain and so easily lost. Be cognizant of this.

5.  Forgive everything and everybody, every time. Do yourself this favor; it will allow you to let go of anger, guilt, and anguish. You may not wish to continue the relationship at hand, but bless it, let it go, and move on. Do not hold on to the negativity; allow the law of karma to take care of it for you.

6.  Spend time in silence, meditation, and prayer daily to commune with Spirit. Have a conversation with God, and get to know your own personal divine posse. Live your truth, speak your truth, and trust that the abundant universe will respond.

7.  Know that you are here in this lifetime with your own special purpose and trajectory. Follow your passion until you find it. You

will know by how you feel and the ease of how it flows that you are moving in the right direction.

8.  Beat your drum with a rhythm all your own. Do not try to emulate others or keep up with them. Do you, for you are your own unique self, and no one can be just like you, just as you cannot be just like them. Stay true to who you are and what makes your heart sing.

9.  Do not waste time on people who make you feel anything other than wonderful and beautiful. Learn to have boundaries. Know that if it feels uncomfortable, there is a reason for it. Listen to your heart, and surround yourself with people, places, and things that enhance you and the quality of your life.

10. Remember: all that is Go(o)d is of God. Anything other than that is ego, trying to (E)dge (G)od (O)ut. It is just that simple.

11. There is a lot of darkness in this world. Be the change you wish to experience. Shine your light, and make a difference, every minute of every day. This is how we, as individuals, can do our part to change the world, one day at a time, one step at a time. Radiate love.

12. Take care of your body, mind, and soul. Eat healthy, and exercise on a regular basis. Stimulate your mind with new and positive information and feed your soul the nourishment it craves by connecting to the divine every day.

13. No matter what, always be the best you can be at any given moment in time. All you ever have is this moment. If you choose

wisely and with good intention, you will never have to live with regret.

14. Keep your surroundings neat, clean, and tidy. The energy that emanates from this will fuel your life with constant positivity.

15. Be accountable for all your words and actions. Take responsibility for yourself. Do not expect others to do it for you. Instead, learn to be independent so you can experience synergy and interdependence in your relationships. This is the basis of healthy relationships.

16. Take a moment and step back when making decisions, knowing that there are consequences for every action and reaction in this life. Choose wisely.

17. Make it a priority to be better today than you were yesterday and better tomorrow than you were today. Each day is a gift; stop and smell the roses.

18. Tell your loved ones daily that you love them. Live in a state of gratitude for all that is bestowed upon you, even if it doesn't seem like much. Your love and gratitude will create abundance, and it will be returned to you tenfold.

19. Live in service to others. There are many ways to give of yourself to your fellow brothers and sisters. It need not cost a dime. The best gift comes from the kindness of your heart; it's priceless.

20. Do everything in your power to keep your life stress-free and balanced, for this creates perfect health. Never keep your emotions in; wear them on your sleeve and have conversations that keep

everything open and on the table. Your life will become a direct reflection of how well you've learned this wisdom.

21. If you are so inclined, travel. Traveling is the best way to understand and gain compassion for different people, places, races, and cultures. Honor the differences, and always have respect for another's world.

22. Respect Mother Nature and take care of our earthly home. Educate yourself on the different ways you can help save the environment. Work in a garden, and commune with nature, taking in her beautiful energy.

23. Make your family number one. They are your people. Strive for harmony in all your familial relationships. Lift them up to be all they can be. Fill them with love, attention, adoration, and appreciation, especially your children; it sets the stage for the rest of their lives.

24. Learn to say, "I'm sorry," and accept apologies from others. Nobody is perfect. We're all here doing the best we can, just trying to get it right. This too shall pass, and the storms are our biggest teachers.

25. Find your community of like-minded people who resonate with your soul. There is a beautiful and humble power that is created when you surround yourself with a group of people who think alike. Use it for all that is Go(o)d.

26. And last but not least, always take care of life, and life will always take care of you. Reciprocity is a universal law. And remember, life

is synonymous with God, and God will always take care of you; it's his promise and his gift to us all.

The journey you take to awakening and enlightenment has many pathways and threads. My hope in writing this book is to open your eyes to the many facets of your spiritual journey, teaching you to trust your innate feelings and the voice within to guide you as you lift the veil, little by little, one baby step at a time. Allow yourself to create a spiritual philosophy that is all your own, based on what feels right and good for you. Then follow the yellow brick road home, home to your personal heaven on earth, living on earth as it is in heaven.

Blessings to you all. Namaste.

One last Message from Love, entitled "In the Silence."

. . . . . . . . . . . . . . . . . . . . . . . . . . . . . . . . . . . . . . . . . . . . . . . . . . . . . . . . . . . . . . . . . . .

## In the Silence

*"My child, you shall find me in the silence and feel me in the silence. For this is where I reside, in the peace that you feel when the world is quiet, when the silence is almost so loud that it fills the room, not with noise but with grace. Peace is my language of the soul. It is like residing in a thick bubble of pure peace and consequently feeling immense joy, the result of which brings an overwhelming emotion of tears, tears filled with joy that well up in your eyes and run down your cheeks. This, my love, is the feeling of my presence in and*

*around you, filling your vessel and the space you occupy. It is an overwhelming and otherworldly feeling. It is distinctly different than the niceties that you may feel on earth. It is so immensely beautiful and overwhelming that you well up with such emotion that it fills your whole body and there's no holding it back. Enjoy this beautiful feeling of my love, joy, and grace. It is, again, my gift for those of you who have found me in their hearts and souls, for those of you who have found me within and connect to my grace."*

> *"Blessed are those who walk in accordance to my word, allowing me to infiltrate their hearts and speak through the voice of babes. My children, walk in life as if no one is watching.*
> *Beat the drum you find only with me.*
> *Love with a heart that is overflowing with the most beautiful emotion.*
> *Trust that which your heart knows to be true and listen to the obscure ways that I speak to you."*

*"Know that when it seems like a miracle, it truly is. This is my way of getting your attention for something you need to know. I truly have earthly angels and messengers. How else could I reach my children and have my messages heard? Not everyone has found my voice within. So blessed are those who hear my voice, for they are my instruments to awaken my children who are still in the darkness of this illusion called life on earth. Find me, feel me, see me in and around the likes of you. Get to know the way it feels when your life is flowing with me. You'll know it because it will feel easy, loving, peaceful, and*

*beautiful; the synchronicities will abound. I love to shower my children with all that is Go(o)d, all that is of me, their loving Father in heaven."*

*"I love you always and forever. Amen."*

· · · · · · · · · · · · · · · · · · · · · · · · · · · · · · · · · · · · · · · · · · · · · · · · · · ·

# The Man Who Climbed to God

## By Eva Belle Werber

The man was told that on the mountaintop he would find God, that there he would meet Him face to face. So the man arose early, before the light of day, and started on his journey. As he climbed, he became thirsty and sought a brook where he could quench his thirst. While resting beside the brook, he fell asleep. As he slept, Spirit came down from the mountaintop; His form was that of a young man, strong of stature, with eyes of piercing beauty.

Spirit spoke. His voice rang out as a clear sweet bell, and these are the words that He said: "You've started the journey of the soul, away from the crowded cities with their glamour and deceit. Away from the rush of life as it is lived by man in his ignorance. You came alone to the mountain trail as day dawned in your consciousness, in quest of what life really means. You entered on the way of the lonely ones, thinking if you kept to the path, up and over the crags of old beliefs and old desires, that at last, you would find Me, God. But I wait not there, in My high place of glory, while you make the journey alone. I saw the desire burning in your heart and hastened down to meet you, so that together we might make the journey back from sense to soul. "The Way", after all, will not be a lonely one, for every step of the way, you shall have celestial companionship. Awake. Rise up. Let us be on our way with joy."

The man awoke and found he had slept through the hours of the day, and the soft evening dew was upon his cheeks. The sky was jeweled with stars. There was a great stillness, and behold, he was upon the mountaintop. He knew that God was there, and within his heart was a great silence, and there, within his heart, dwelt God. He sang with joy, for he had found a great secret: that where there is stillness within, there can God always be found.

So he spent the night on the mountaintop in quiet meditation, and with the day's dawning, he went down the trail to the busy city. This time, God went with him, and the man walked and talked with Spirit as they strolled down the busy city streets.

He was filled with peace, for he had found that the mountaintop was his own soul's awakening at last to the reality of its true being, and never again would he have to search to find God.

# AFTERWORD

We all have a personal agenda when we incarnate into this life. Life on earth is a school of learning through opposites. Where you come from in the nonphysical realm of pure unconditional love, peace, and compassion, you understand that this earthly life is an opportunity to grow your soul spiritually. When you incarnate, you advance through tangible experiences that are gained during this particularly difficult teaching method. It takes immense courage and bravery to decide to come into a life on earth, considering we have no memory of who we really are or our infinite, innate capabilities. Consequently, you spend your whole life navigating through the forest, longing to see the trees and looking for a glimpse of light to shine through. The experiences you have in your formative years, your childhood, generally shape the rest of your life. This gives you the opportunity to reflect back on the personal circumstances of your upbringing, which give you a clue as to what lessons you chose to experience for this incarnation.

Without exception, there is a reason you chose to be here. These experiences plummet you forward into adulthood, where you act out what you experienced in childhood. Be it positive or negative, you can be assured that what shows up is always an opportunity to learn, grow, and balance karma in the specific areas of your choosing. The clincher to this concept is that you have free will, which gives you choices. Through these choices, you have experiences. These experiences always create a feeling.

Feelings are our gift for so bravely choosing the earth school way of learning. We navigate through our lives by the way things make us feel. There are feelings in our gut that are always present. It's a matter of creating awareness and a relationship with this part of your self. As you tune in, have enough experiences that teach you to listen to it, you gain strength through this process. As you continue on and listen more intently to it, you start the process of healing the past, growing into becoming, and eventually arrive at an awareness that there is much more going on in this life than meets the eye. You go deeper within and gain an awareness that you are a spirit and a soul, housed in this human suit called a body. The body is just the vehicle that allows you to learn and grow in this school called earth.

If we all understood that everything and everybody gives us an opportunity learn and grow, and that there is surely a silver lining in every experience without exception, we could successfully achieve the goals we set out to accomplish when making the brave decision to incarnate into life on earth. You have an opportunity to create anything of your choosing as you navigate with a perspective that is loving, kind, and compassionate. When your perspective sees with eyes of love and compassion, you experience the gift of peace. Peace should always be the end goal with anything and everything you experience. The journey we call life requires learning how to navigate to have your endgame become peace.

This book is not intended to be the source of all information, but a tool to help spark an awakening within you that drives your personal quest to start your own spiritual journey, where you can create a philosophy and truth that comes from your own heart and soul. May your thirst for the truth be quenched by the yearning that has been sparked within your soul.

# SUGGESTED BOOKS AND AUTHORS

The following resources have been a source of inspiration to me:

Wayne Dyer

Eva Belle Werber

Gary Zukav

Neal Donald Walsh

Oprah Winfrey's *Super Soul Sunday*

Doreen Virtue

Delores Cannon

Thomas Charles Sannar

Brian Weiss

Deepak Chopra

Eckhart Tolle

Louise Hay

Stephen Covey

Og Mandingo

Marianne Williamson

Kenneth Wapnick

*A Course in Miracles*

Anita Majori

Lorna Byrne

Sylvia Brown

John Edwards

Don Miguel Ruiz

Dr. Phil McGraw

Kathleen McGowan

Simran Singh

Annie Kirkwood

James Twyman

Mike Dooley

Barbara DeAngelis

Jean-Yves Leloup

Ariadne Green

Anaiya Sophia

Dan Millman

Anthony William

Gary Smalley

# ABOUT THE BOOK

*Messages from Love* is a book based on a spiritual podcast exploring the concept that we are all directly connected to God. It offers an understanding that love and forgiveness are the way to living a peaceful and joy-filled life. This book represents Connie Cord's personal spiritual journey and awakening. Connie was inspired to write the messages that came forth in her meditative state each morning. She then transformed these writings into a thirteen-episode podcast, which she collaborated on with her niece. These words of wisdom are now reflected in this book. They are beautiful and profound messages that she believes are directly channeled through her connection with God, or what some may understand to be their higher self or the voice of the Holy Spirit.

Each chapter builds upon the next, giving you the opportunity to create a philosophy of your own that will resonate personally with you and change the lens you view life with in the most beautiful and positive way.

# ABOUT THE AUTHOR

Connie Cord was born in Portland, Oregon, raised in Northern California by wonderful parents, and ultimately made her home in California's Bay Area, since 1984. Married in her early twenties, she was blessed with the opportunity to become the mother of a beautiful daughter, who has since gifted her with two adorable grandchildren. Divorced in her late twenties, Connie set out in life as a single working mother to find her way as an aesthetician by trade; her skin care business flourished for over thirty years. Connie has always enjoyed her designated career with a personal mission of making her clients look and feel beautiful, inside and out. Her true passion in life, however, has been the study of spirituality and the divine realm. She's always searching for her own personal truth and is an avid truth-seeker on a constant spiritual quest. Through her own personal experiences, reading books from a variety of spiritual authors, and attending numerous seminars, she has found her own direct connection to the divine. *Messages from Love* is the culmination of her diverse studies all wrapped up together, creating her own personal spiritual philosophy.